JAMAICA BAY ARTIFACTS

JAMAICA BAY PAMPHLET LIBRARY 12

JAMAICA BAY ARTIFACTS

STRUCTURES OF COASTAL RESILIENCE

Jamaica Bay Team
Spitzer School of Architecture
The City College of New York

Catherine Seavitt Nordenson, editor
Associate Professor of Landscape Architecture

Kjirsten Alexander
Research Associate

Danae Alessi
Research Associate

Eli Sands
Research Assistant

JAMAICA BAY PAMPHLET LIBRARY
12 Jamaica Bay Artifacts

ISBN 978-1-942900-12-2

CONTACT
Catherine Seavitt Nordenson
cseavittnordenson@ccny.cuny.edu
www.structuresofcoastalresilience.org

SCR Jamaica Bay Team
The City College of New York
Spitzer School of Architecture
Program in Landscape Architecture, Room 2M24A
141 Convent Avenue New York, New York 10031

COVER
Beach at Dead Horse Bay.
photo: Kjirsten Alexander

The artifacts pictured in this pamphlet have been cataloged and archived by the NPS Gateway National Recreation Area's Department of Cultural Resources, Fort Wadsworth, Staten Island.

supported by

Horse Bone

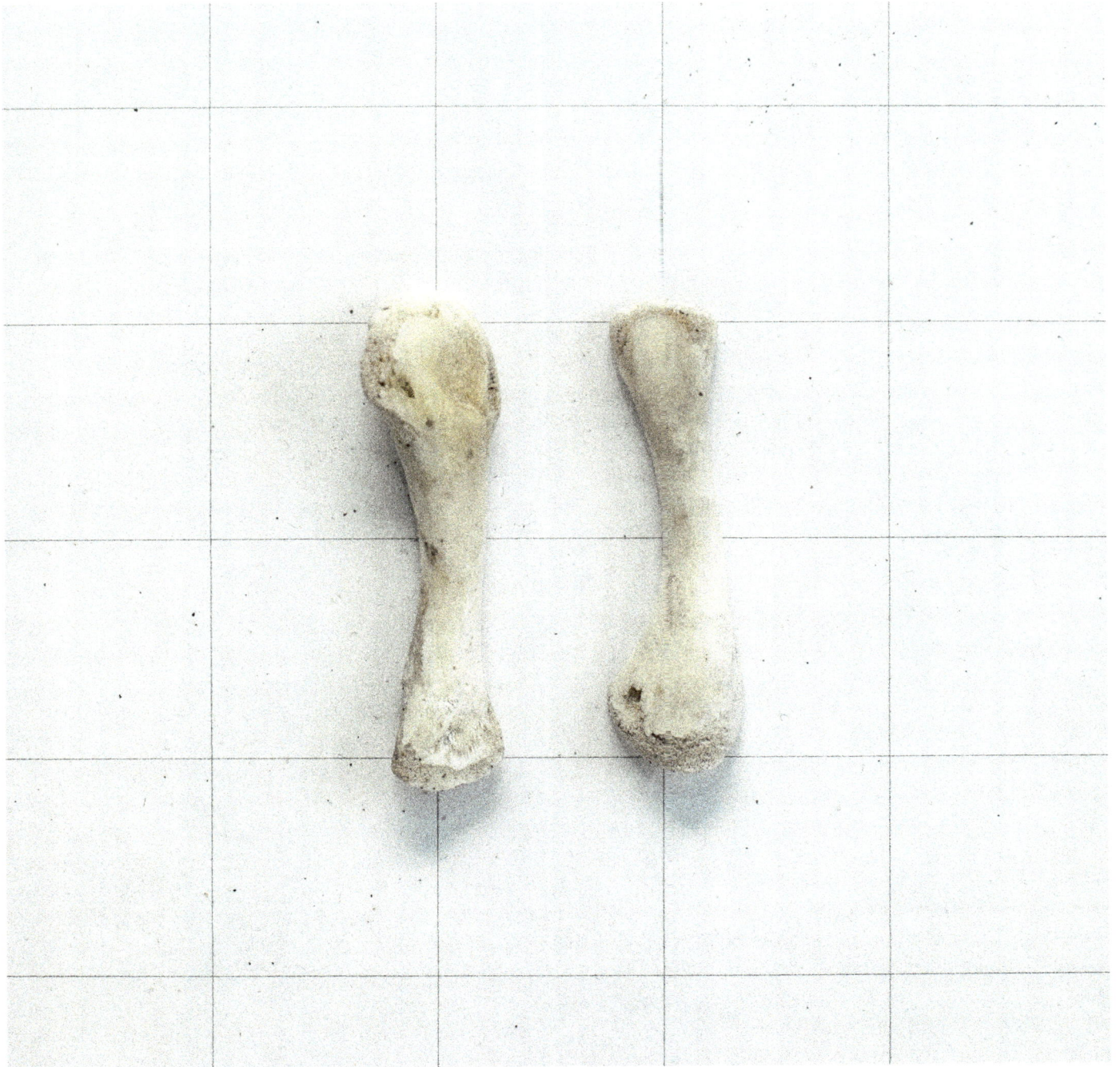

Bird Bones

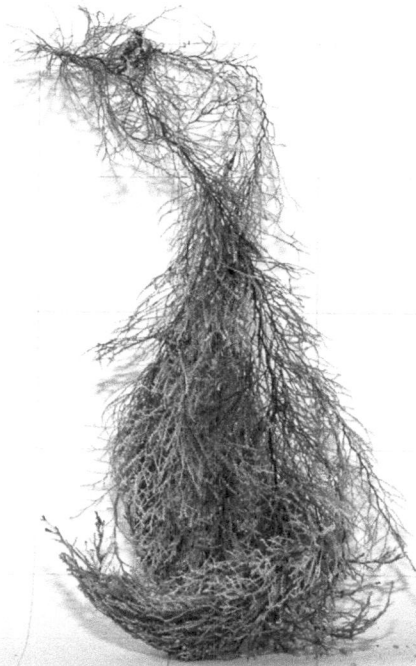

Dried Sea Weed

9

Channeled Whelk Shell (view A)

Channeled Whelk Shell (view B)

Horse Bone (view A)

Horse Bone (view B)

Softshell Clam Shell

Atlantic Surfclam Shell

Oyster Shell (view A)

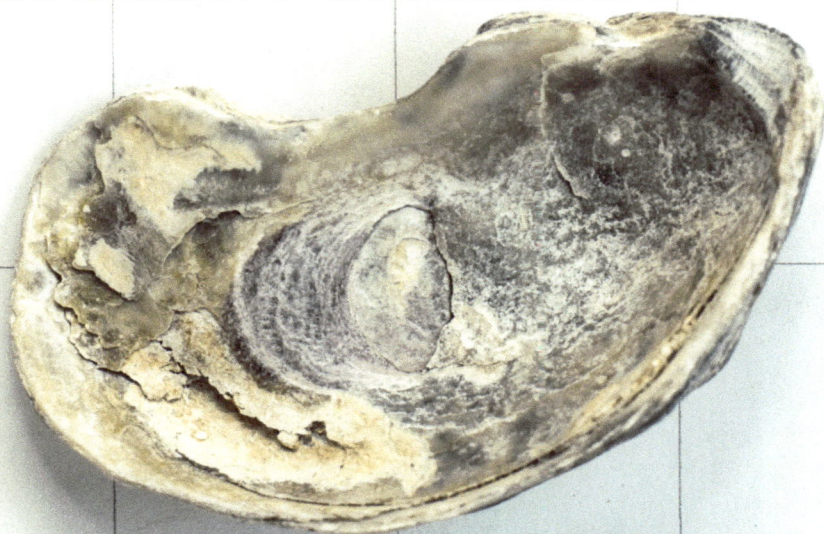

Oyster Shell (view B)

"ASTRING-O-SOL" Glass Bottle with Sand and Water (front)

"ASTRING-O-SOL" Glass Bottle with Sand and Water (side)

16

Three Glass Bottles

Glass Bottle with Sand

Three Glass Bottles

Glass Bottle

Tall Glass Bottle

Three Brown Bottles

Steel Bowl

Green Glass Bottle Bottom

Brown Sea Glass

"Noxema" Blue Sea Glass

Green Sea Glass

Clear Sea Glass

Brown Pottery Shard

Clay Offering Vessel

Clay Offering Vessel with String

Brown Sea Glass

Plastic Cap

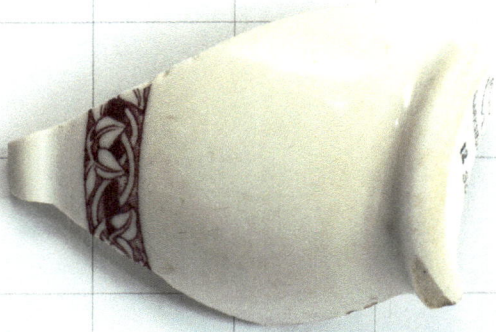

Clarksburg Pottery Shard (view A)

Clarksburg Pottery Shard (view B)

Royal Pottery Shard (view A)

Royal Pottery Shard (view B)

Cape Cod Pottery Shard (view A)

Cape Cod Pottery Shard (view B)

Turquoise Pottery Shard (view A)

Turquoise Pottery Shard (view B)

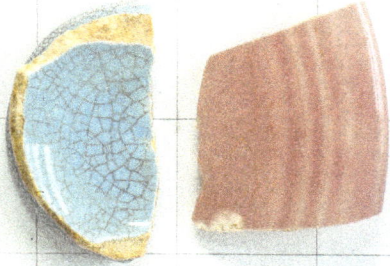

Blue and Pink Pottery Shards

Green Pottery Shard

Green Pottery Shard

Blue Pottery Shard

Yellow and Blue Pottery Shards

28

Blue and White Pottery Shard, Made in Occupied Japan

Blue and White Pottery Shard

Blue and White Pottery Shard

Blue and White Pottery Shard

Red and White Pottery Shard

Floral Pottery Shard

Garden Pottery Shard

Floral Pottery Shard

Blue and Brown Pottery Shard

Ceramic Floor Tiles

Blue Pottery Shard (view A)

Blue Pottery Shard (view B)

Mesh Coin Purse

Steel Washer

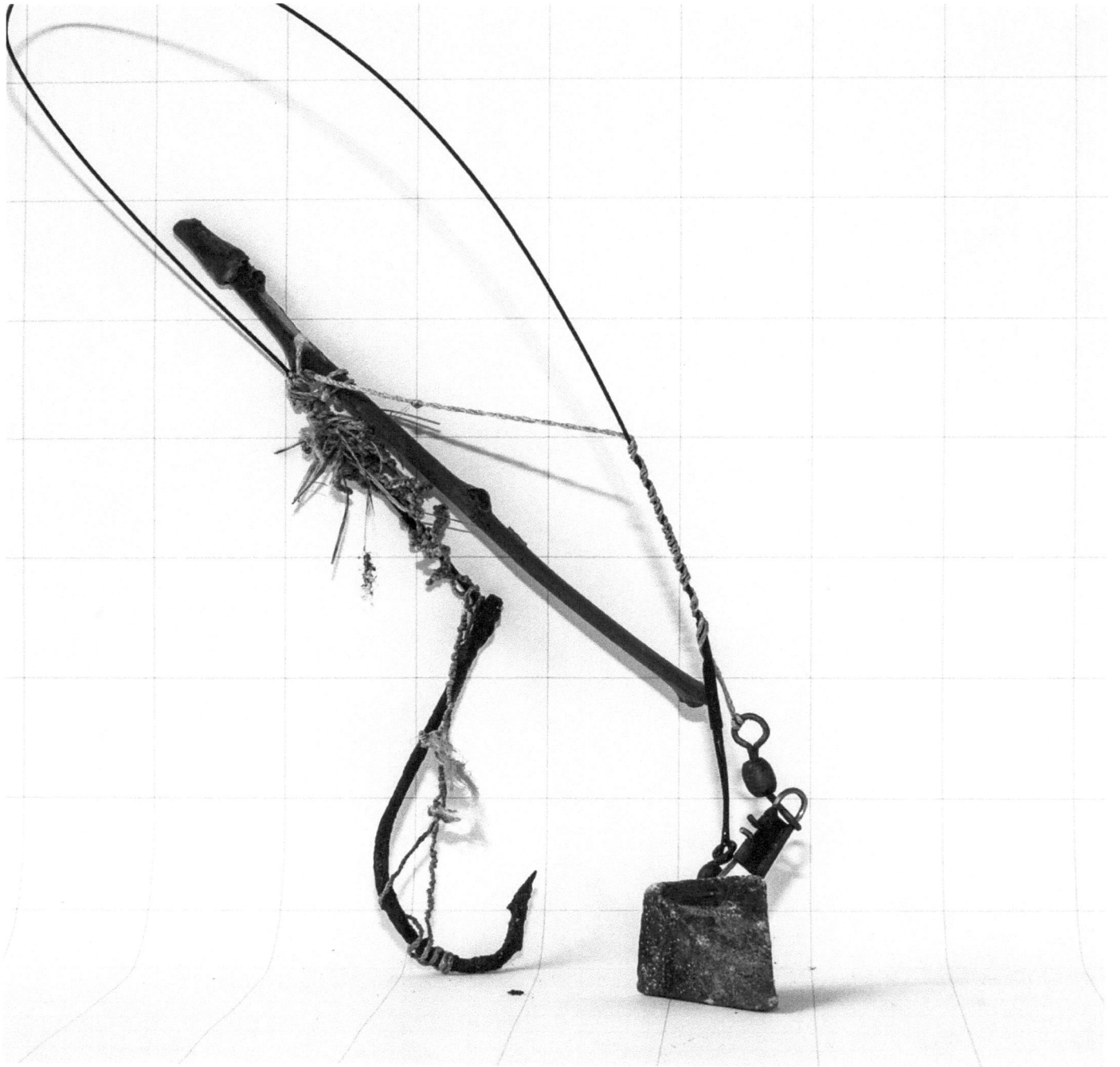

Hook and Sink

Artifacts pictured were collected by the City College of
New York Jamaica Bay SCR Research Team at Dead
Horse Bay, the West Pond of the Jamaica Bay Wildlife
Refuge, and Spring Creek Park, New York, 2013-2014,
and photographed with one-inch grid background by Eli
Sands, August 2014. The artifacts pictured in this pamphlet
have been cataloged and archived by the National Park
Service Gateway National Recreation Area's Department
of Cultural Resources, Fort Wadsworth, Staten Island.

www.ingramcontent.com/pod-product-compliance
Lightning Source LLC
Chambersburg PA
CBHW060827270326
41931CB00002B/84